Jokes &
Riddles

Critter

Janet Nuzum Myers

Illustrated by
Dave Clegg

Jokes & Riddles

STERLING

New York / London

www.sterlingpublishing.com/kids

STERLING and the distinctive Sterling logo are registered trademarks of
Sterling Publishing Co., Inc.

Library of Congress Cataloging-in-Publication Data

Myers, Janet Nuzum
  Critter jokes & riddles / Janet Nuzum Myers ; illustrated by Dave Clegg.
      p. cm.
  Includes index.
  ISBN-13: 978-1-4027-3865-4
  ISBN-10: 1-4027-3865-X
  1. Animals--Juvenile humor. 2. Riddles, Juvenile. I. Title.
      II. Title: Critter jokes and riddles.

PN6231.A5M94 2007
818'.60208--dc22

                                    2007003246

10   9   8   7   6   5   4   3   2

Published by Sterling Publishing Co., Inc.
387 Park Avenue South, New York, NY 10016
© 2007 by Janet Myers
Illustrations © 2007 by Dave Clegg
Distributed in Canada by Sterling Publishing
^c/o Canadian Manda Group, 165 Dufferin Street
Toronto, Ontario, Canada M6K 3H6
Distributed in the United Kingdom by GMC Distribution Services
Castle Place, 166 High Street, Lewes, East Sussex, England BN7 1XU
Distributed in Australia by Capricorn Link (Australia) Pty. Ltd.
P.O. Box 704, Windsor, NSW 2756, Australia

Sterling ISBN 978-1-4027-3865-4

For information about custom editions, special sales, premium and corporate
purchases, please contact Sterling Special Sales Department at 800-805-5489
or specialsales@sterlingpublishing.com.

Contents

1
Critters that Swim

Why are whales considered sad?
Because they are blubbery.

What do you call a daddy whale?
The podfather.

What's the difference between a humpback and a guppy?
  A whale of a difference.

What happens if a whale eats too much?
  He'll sink or swim.

How do whales stretch the truth?
  They tell fishy stories.

What's gray and has a tail and a trunk?
  A whale on vacation.

When do whales get into trouble?
  When they spout off.

What's a fish's favorite country?
  Finland.

Why do fish avoid computers?
  They get caught in the Internet.

What do you get if you cross a fish and a Harley?
  A motor pike.

What game do young salmon play?
  "Salmon Says."

What do you call a cowboy squid?
Billy the Squid.

Why is a squid considered sweet?
Because it has lots of suckers.

What fish get married?
Sole mates.

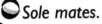

3

What fish does not like to be alone?
  A grouper.

What's the nicest fish?
  An angelfish.

What fish works in a hospital?
  A sturgeon.

What do you call sunbathing fish?
  A fish fry.

What fish comes out at night?
  A starfish.

What fish is a bad swimmer?
  A flounder.

What fish goes to church?
  A holy mackerel.

Why are fish so smart?
  Because they live in schools.

What grades do fish get in school?
  They are below "C" level.

How do you communicate with fish?
  Drop them a line.

Why did the fish bite a hook?
  It was lured.

What's an Olympic event for fish?
  The fishing pole vault.

What did the fish say to his old friend?
  "Long time no sea."

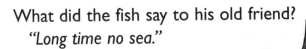

5

Why was the fish sick?
He cod a cold.

What do you get if you cross a cod and a potato?
Fish-and-chips.

Why was the fish sore?
He pulled a mussel.

Why was the fish tired?
He was swimming against the tide.

Where do fish sell their jewelry?
At the prawn shop.

When do seals giggle?
When they hear seal-y jokes.

Why is it hard to fool a seal?
They can smell something fishy.

What do seals do with a love letter?
Seal it with a kiss.

How do seals keep secrets?
Their lips are sealed.

6

What do you call a funny seal?
Lu-seal Ball.

What seal is musical?
A harp seal.

What do you call a shark in the desert?
A fish out of water.

What do you get if you cross a shark and
a computer?
Lots of bites.

What do you get if you cross the Loch Ness Monster and a shark?
Loch Jaws.

What do you call sunbathing clams?
A clambake.

Why do lobsters refuse to share?
Because they are shellfish.

What position did the lobster play on the baseball team?
Pinch hitter.

2
Critters with Fur

What do you call a hairless bear?
A bare bear.

Why was the baby bear digging in the ground?
He wanted to make a cubbyhole.

What do you call toothless bears?
Gummy bears.

Why don't bears have New Year's Eve parties?
Because they are hibernating!

What do you call an annoying bear?
Un-bear-able.

Why don't bears wear hats?
They like being bear-headed.

Where do you find German bears?
Bear-lin.

What do polite bears say?
"Thank you beary much."

Why did the bear attend a wedding?
He was the ring bear.

What do you call a bear on a rainy day?
A drizzly bear.

Why did the bear put evergreen trees in her den?
She wanted to spruce up the place.

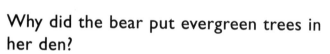

What's an Australian bear's favorite city?
Can-bear-a.

Why did the man jump on a bear?
He was a bear-back rider.

What can leap tall buildings in a single bound?
A kangaroo on a trampoline.

What do you call a tired kangaroo?
Out of bounds.

What do you call a kangaroo that watches TV all day?
A pouch potato.

What do you get if you cross a kangaroo and a male deer?
A buckaroo.

What's a polar bear's favorite food?
  Iceburgers.

Where do bears go on vacation?
  Bear-muda.

What do you call a toy bear in a snowstorm?
  A teddy brrrr.

Why can't you feed a teddy bear?
  Because it's already stuffed.

Why do bears get cold?
  Because they have bear feet.

What do you get if you cross a bear
and a skunk?
  Winnie the Phew!

What do you call a wolf wearing
a wool sweater?
  A wolf in sheep's clothing.

Why do wolves have bad table manners?
  Because they wolf down their food.

Where do wolves get new tails?
At the retail shop.

What side of a mink has the most fur?
The outside.

What do you get if you cross a mink
and an octopus?
A fur coat with eight arms.

How does a mink keep warm?
With its fur-nace.

How did the mink escape?
It ran fur away.

What does a polite mink say?
Thank you furry much.

The mink promised to love his wife
for how long?
Furever.

What are minks' favorite flowers?
Fur-get-me-nots.

What do you do if a gorilla sneezes?
Get out of the way.

If you throw a gorilla into the water,
what will it become?
 Wet. (And you should run!)

What did the gorilla say to her son?
 "Stop monkeying around."

How do you make a gorilla stew?
 Keep it waiting for an hour.

What big, hairy animal plays soccer?
 A goal-rilla.

What's a gorilla's favorite fruit?
Ape-ricots.

What's an ape's favorite cookie?
Chocolate chimp.

Why did the young ape act like his father?
He was a chimp off the old block.

What do you get if you cross a chimp
and a tuna?
Fish and chimps.

What do you call a cat at the North Pole?
A polecat.

What's red and has black and white stripes?
An embarrassed skunk.

How do you keep a skunk from smelling?
Hold its little nose.

What did the courtroom judge say
to the skunk?
"Odor in the court!"

How do mice spread gossip?
By word of mouse.

What do you call mice in a freezer?
  Mice cubes.

Why was a mouse stuck on a man's face?
  It was a mouse-tache.

Why did the mouse stay indoors?
  Because it was raining cats and dogs.

How do mice welcome a new neighbor?
  They have a mousewarming party.

What do you call a great painting
by an artistic mouse?
  A mousterpiece.

MORE 3
Critters with Fur

What kind of motorbike does a rabbit ride?
A Yamahoppy.

Where does a rabbit catch a plane?
At the hareport.

What's a young bunny's favorite game?
  Hopscotch.

What do you get if you cross a rabbit with a ghost?
  Nothing to look at.

What do you say to a hitchhiker rabbit?
  "Hop in."

How did the rabbit win the race?
  He won by a hare.

What game do rabbits play in the winter?
  Ice hoppy.

What did the mole say to her son?
  "Where in earth have you been?"

What do you get if you cross a chicken
and a puppy?
  The chick of the litter.

What do you call a poodle in a clothes dryer?
  A Whirlpoodle.

What happened when witches adopted a
friendly dog?
  He went from wags to witches.

19

What's a young dog's favorite food?
Pup-peroni pizza.

Why do dogs hang out at railroad stations?
So they can be trained.

What do you get if you cross a bloodhound
and a locomotive?
A search engine.

What do you call a vehicle for dogs?
A muttercycle.

What's a young dog's favorite candy?
Pup-per-mints.

What did the baseball-player puppy want
to be someday?
A dog catcher.

What did the dog say to his girlfriend?
"You look fetching tonight."

What do you call luggage for dogs?
Doggie bags.

What do you call young dogs romping
in the snow?
Slush puppies.

What do you call a dog at the equator?
  A hot dog.

How do dogs greet each other?
  "Howl are you?"

What do you call a dog that runs marathons?
  Dog tired.

What do you call an automobile for dogs?
  Waggin' wheels.

Where did the dog leave his car?
  In the barking lot.

What do you get if you cross a chipmunk
and an Airedale?
  Chip 'n Dale.

What dog always knows the time?
  A watchdog.

How did dogs travel in the Old West?
  In waggin' trains.

What's a dog groomer's slogan?
  Hair today, gone tomorrow.

What did the dog say to his girlfriend?
  "I ruff you."

What do you get if you cross a dog
and an aardvark?
  An arf-bark.

What's another name for Yorkshire
terrier puppies?
  New Yorkers.

What do you get if you cross a crocodile and a dog?
  A crocker spaniel.

What do you get if you cross a fox
and a monster?
  A fox terror.

What do you call a flower-sniffing dog?
  A budhound.

Why was the dog in lots of fights?
  He was a Boxer.

What's a popular honeymoon spot for dogs?
Niagara Paws.

Where do party dogs ride on floats?
At the Mardi Growl.

What's a dog's favorite holiday?
Howl-o-ween.

What's an Italian dog's favorite food?
Paw-sta.

How did the dog become a hero?
He let the cat out of the bag.

What do you call a dog in the mud?
A dirty dog.

4
Cold-Blooded Critters

Why do frogs smile?
Because they are hoppy.

Why did two frogs cling to the front of a car?
They wanted to be froglights.

What do you get if you cross a crocodile
and a frog?
   A croak-a-dile.

What do you say to a frog on the first of January?
   "Hoppy New Year!"

What do frogs eat in France?
French flies.

What do you say to a one-year-old frog?
"Hoppy Birthday."

What do frogs like to drink?
Croak-a-Cola and hot croak-o.

What do you get if you cross a frog and air pollution?
Kermit the Smog.

Where did the frog leave his coat?
In the croakroom.

Why can't frogs enter races?
Because they jump the gun.

What's a frog's motto?
Put on a hoppy face.

What's a frog's favorite year?
Leap year.

What advice do frogs get?
Look before you leap.

Who examines frogs' eyes?
The hop-tometrist.

What's green on the inside and purple
on the outside?
A frog in a purple dress.

What do you call a frog that wins the lottery?
Hoppy go lucky.

What do you call a movie about a frog spy?
A croak and dagger film.

Why did the frog go to the doctor?
He felt jumpy.

Why did the frog accept a new job?
It was a good hopportunity.

Where do frogs cash checks?
At the riverbank.

What games do young frogs play?
Leap frog and croak-quet.

What's a frog's favorite music?
Hip-hop, of course.

What do you call a toad ballerina?
   A toad dancer.

What's a toad's favorite movie?
   Star Warts.

Why wasn't the toad hurt when he fell off
a 30-foot ladder?
   Because he fell off the bottom rung.

Where do you find toads in Poland?
In Wartsaw.

What's a toad after it's six weeks old?
Seven weeks old.

What kind of shoes do toads wear?
Open-toad sandals.

What does a toad wear at a construction site?
Steel-toad boots.

What's a toad's favorite book?
Warts and Peace.

What game do young toads play?
Tic tac toad.

What do you get if you cross a toad
and a tow truck?
A towed toad.

What did the toad say when his girlfriend
asked if he loved her?
"Toadly."

What do you call nervous toads?
Worry warts.

What happened to the turtle that was struck
by lightning?
He was shell-shocked.

What do you call a turtle in a hot tub?
Turtle soup.

What was the turtle doing on the highway?
About one mile a day.

What do you get if you cross a turtle
and a sheep?
A wool turtleneck.

What did the turtle name her daughter?
Shelly.

How do you greet a turtle with three heads?
"Hello, hello, hello."

Why do turtles never forget?
Because they have turtle recall.

Why are turtles never homeless?
They have permanent shell-ters.

What do you call a turtle basketball team in Massachusetts?
The Boston Shelltics.

What happened to the turtle that ate a spoon?
He couldn't stir.

What's a good gift for a turtle?
A shellular phone.

What do you call a turtle that plays with dynamite?
A bombshell.

SCARY
5
Cold-Blooded Critters

What elderly reptile knows how to tell time?
A grandfather croc.

Why was the crocodile unable to sing?
He had a frog in his throat.

What do you call an alligator that volunteers its help?
Gator aid.

What reptile is the first one up each morning?
The alarm croc.

What do you call a nutty crocodile?
A cuckoo croc.

What's a good gift for a crocodile chef?
A crock pot.

What do you get if you cross
a lizard and a snowman?
   A blizzard.

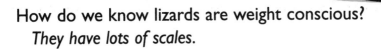

What's a reptile's favorite movie?
   The Lizard of Oz.

How do we know lizards are weight conscious?
   They have lots of scales.

Where do rich lizards live?
   In up-scale neighborhoods.

What do you call a lizard at the North Pole?
   Lost.

How did the lizard start a business?
   He started on a small scale.

How do lizards climb mountains?
   They scale them.

What's long, thin, and green underneath?
   A snake in the grass.

At a rattlesnakes' race, what does the starter say?
   "Snakes, rattle and roll!"

What does a snake call the snake he's dating?
His coilfriend.

How is a snake like steam?
They both say "Sssss."

What goes slither, slither, hop, slither, slither, hop?
A snake with hiccups.

What do you call a snake that can't stop laughing?
Hiss-terical.

What game do snakes play?
  Sssss-occer.

How do snakes monogram their towels?
  Hiss and hers.

What do you call a snake that has
a government job?
  A civil serpent.

Why did the snake lose arguments?
  Because he didn't have a leg to stand on.

What subject does a snake study in school?
  Hiss-tory.

What snake has bad table manners?
  A spitting cobra.

What do you get if you cross a snake
and a groundhog?
  An animal too thin to see its own shadow.

What snake knows how to dance?
  A Mamba.

What snake is good at math?
  An Adder.

What snake is always thirsty?
   A Cottonmouth.

What snakes wear soggy shoes?
   Water Moccasins.

What snake can stretch the most?
   A Garter snake.

What snake wears a badge?
   A Copperhead.

What do you get if you cross a snake and a bird?
   A Feather Boa.

Why can't you fool a snake?
   Because you can't pull its leg.

What did the Boa Constrictor say to the mouse?
   "I'm squeezed to meet you."

What's a Boa Constrictor's motto?
   "You can't squeeze everyone."

How many Pythons can fit into an elevator?
   No one knows—they always squeeze in one more.

How do Pythons and Boa Constrictors
play baseball?
They make lots of squeeze plays.

What sign is posted at a Boa Constrictors'
family reunion?
"No hugging!"

What did the Boa Constrictor say to the Python?
"I've got a crush on you."

What snake builds houses?
A Boa Constructor.

What did the Python say after eating too much?
"I feel sss-queasy."

Why didn't the Python buy a new dress?
She couldn't squeeze into it.

What do you get if you cross a Python and an orange?
Fresh-squeezed orange juice.

What do you call a huge reptile that falls down?
A dino-sore.

What huge reptiles ate lemons?
Dino-sours.

What do you call a dinosaur with an explosive temper?
Dino-mite.

What do you do if you find a dinosaur in your bed?
Sleep on the sofa.

What do you call a dinosaur with a large vocabulary?
Thesaurus Rex.

What did the T-Rex do on his birthday?
Anything he wanted to do.

What do you call a dinosaur that delivers packages?
Fed Rex.

What huge reptile sleeps a lot?
A dino-snore.

What time is it when a dinosaur sits
on your sofa?
Time to get a new sofa.

6
BIG & Small Cat Critters

What do you call a lion on a football team?
The lionbacker.

Where do you find lions in a small town?
On Mane Street.

What did the movie star lion win?
  An A-catemy A-roared.

What do you call lions dancing
in a single file?
  Lion dancers.

What do you call circus lions?
  The mane event.

How did the motorist wind up in the hospital?
  He crossed double lions.

How do lions travel?
  They fly on air-lions.

Why did the tiger wear a judge's robe?
  He was the law of the jungle.

What do you do with a blue tiger?
  Cheer him up.

When do tigers have eight legs?
  When there are two of them.

Why did the tiger carry an antenna
to her wedding?
  So her reception would be good.

What happened to the leopard that fell into a washing machine?
He came out spotless.

What did the leopard say, after eating?
"That hit the spots."

What's the best way to call a leopard?
Long distance.

Why can't leopards play hide and seek?
Because they are always spotted.

What's spotted and bouncy?
A leopard on a pogo stick.

How did the leopard change her spots?
She moved.

Where do leopards, cheetahs, and lions meet for dinner?
At the corner beastro.

Which big cats can't be trusted?
Lions and cheetahs.

What do you call an upper-class cat?
An aristo-cat.

How does a cat make a sweater?
Knit one, purr two….

What happened to the cat that met a porcupine?
Curiosity quilled the cat.

What happened when the cat jumped
into a freezer?
Curiosity chilled the cat.

Why did the cat read books?
She was very litter-ary.

How did the cat celebrate her kitten's birthday?
She gave a big purrty.

Where do cats shop?
In cat-alogs.

Why did the cat dress like a nurse?
She was the first-aid kit-ty.

What score did the cat get on his math test?
Purr-fect.

How can you tell when a cat has been eating dog food?
He starts chasing cars.

What game do kittens play?
Mewsical chairs.

What do you call a five-day-old cat in China?
A kitten.

What do you call writing paper for a cat?
A scratch pad.

Where do you find Hawaiian cats?
Meow-i.

What do you call a stray cat at a dog show?
A cat-astrophe.

Where do cats keep their clothes?
In claw-sets.

What kind of car does a cat drive?
A Catillac.

Who gives cats presents?
Santa Claws.

Why do cats avoid elevators?
They are claws-trophobic.

Why are cats careful after a rainstorm?
They don't want to step in a poodle.

What do cats eat at birthday parties?
Cake and mice cream.

How do cats find out about current events?
They read the mewspapers.

What did the cat say when he played leapfrog with a porcupine?
"Ouch!"

7
Critters with Hooves

Why did the millionaire pig roll in the mud?
He wanted to be filthy rich.

Why did the pig hire a maid?
Because his home looked like a pig sty.

What do pigs say when making a toast
at celebrations?
  "Here's mud in your eye."

What's a pig's favorite pastime?
  Mud slinging.

What do you call a very skinny pig?
  A stick in the mud.

Why do pigs get thrown out of games?
  Because they play dirty.

What do pigs rub on sore muscles?
  Oinkment.

What do you do with a sick pig?
  Call a hambulance.

What do you get if you cross a pig
and a monster?
  A hamster.

Why didn't the pig like her date?
  Because he was a boar.

What ballet is performed by pigs?
  Swine Lake.

Why can't pigs dance?
Because they have two left feet.

What do you call a government official for pigs?
The hambassador.

Why did the pig want to be an actor?
He was a big ham.

Why did the pig claim to be an actor?
  Because his leg was in a cast.

What do you call a sneak attack on a pig?
  A hambush.

Where do you find pigs in Las Vegas?
  At the slop machines.

What do you get if you cross a pig
and a centipede?
  Bacon and legs.

What do you call a karate expert pig?
  A pork chop-er.

Why do pigs go to restaurants?
  To pig out.

Why can't pigs keep secrets?
  Because they squeal.

How do pigs write?
  With pig pens.

Why can't pigs follow directions?
  Because they are pig-headed.

52

What do you call a very important pig?
Big Wig Pig.

Why was the pig a bad driver?
He was a road hog.

What do you call a large pig taking a bath?
Hogwash.

Where do pigs keep their money?
In piggy banks.

What did the piggy bank say to his son?
"Do you think I'm made of money?"

What do you get if you cross a pig and a skeleton?
Hambones.

What did the pig say before getting a shave?
"Bye-bye hair of my chinny-chin-chin."

What play do pigs stay away from?
Hamlet.

What's a pig's favorite state?
New Pork.

Where do city pigs live?
In styscrapers.

What do you get if you cross a pig
and a storyteller?
A pigtail.

What do you call a heavy pig?
A porky porker.

What do you get if you cross a pig and a tree?
A porkypine.

What's a pig's favorite dog?
Porkshire terrier.

What's another name for a nerdy pig?
Dorky porky.

Where do sheep get shaves?
In the baa-baa shop.

Why did the sheep stand in the corner?
Because he'd been baa-d.

What do you call purple sheep?
Dyed in the wool.

What's a sheep's favorite state?
Alabaa-ma.

Why are sheep good at baseball?
They know how to baa-t.

Where do you find young Italian sheep?
In Mi-lamb, Italy.

How do sheep get clean?
They take a baa-th.

What did the polite sheep say?
"How are ewe?"

What's a young sheep's favorite dessert?
Key lamb pie.

Where do sheep go on vacation?
The Baa-hamas.

Why are goats considered rude?
Because they keep butting in.

What do you feed a goat?
Braaa-d and butt-er.

What do you feed a llama?
Llama beans.

How does a llama travel to a prom?
In a llama-sine.

What do you call a play about a mother llama in an emergency room?
Mama llama trauma drama.

57

TALL 8
Critters with Hooves

What did the traffic cop tell the
illegally parked cow?
  "Moo-ve it!"

What sign is posted at an intersection for deer?
  The buck stops here.

What do you call a male deer's money?
Buck's bucks.

When is a buck considered poor?
When he has no doe.

What did the doe say when she saw her new baby?
"Fawn-tastic!"

What type of books do baby deer enjoy?
Fawntasies.

What does a cow wear in Hawaii?
A moo-moo.

Why did the cow keep away from the other cows?
She thought it was better to be seen and not herd.

Why wouldn't the cow stop crying?
She was just milking the situation.

How do you entertain a cow?
Take her to the moo-vies.

What do you call panhandling cattle?
Bum steers.

59

Where do cows win prizes?
  At the Cow-ty Fair.

Where do young cows have lunch?
  In the calf-eteria.

What do you get if you cross a cow and
a pogo stick?
  A milkshake.

What's a cow's favorite city?
Moo-ami, Florida.

What's a cow's favorite state?
Cow-ifornia.

What's a cow's second favorite state?
Moo-souri.

What's a cow's third favorite state?
Moo Jersey.

What do you call cows that borrow money?
Moo-chers.

What's a good gift for a cow?
A lawn moo-er.

What do you get if you cross a cow, a fish,
and a football player?
A Moo-ami Dolphin.

Why was the cow frowning?
She was in a bad mooo-d.

61

What do you get from an Alaskan cow?
Ice cream.

What do you call cows in Alaska?
Eskimoos.

What do you call a cow that works in a bank?
A cash cow.

Why are cows good at math?
They know how to cow-nt.

What do you get if you cross a cow and a mouse?
A moose.

Why did the cow think her new surroundings seemed familiar?
She was experiencing "déjà moo."

What did the cow teach her calf?
Honor thy fodder and thy mudder.

What's a boy calf's favorite sandwich?
Bull-oney.

Where did the young calf meet her friend?
At the corner calf-ay.

What did the calf want to be when she grew up?
A rock moosician.

Why can't bulls get credit cards?
They charge too much.

What do you call sleeping male cattle?
Bulldozers.

63

How do you steer a bull?
Take the bull by the horns.
(But be prepared to run away!)

Why did the cow pack her belongings?
She wanted to moove.

How did she move?
In a mooving van.

What do you call angry male cattle?
Troubulls.

What do you call sweet and friendly male cattle?
Love-abulls.

How do cows count?
With cowculators.

What did the cow say to the comedian?
"You are so amoosing."

What's a cow's favorite book?
Winnie the Moo.

What's a horse's favorite book?
Whinney the Pooh.

What do you call a horse with a sore throat?
A hoarse horse.

What's a young horse's favorite holiday?
April Foals' Day.

What's a horse's favorite game?
Horseshoes, of course.

Why was the colt unable to speak?
Because he was a little horse.

What do you feed a race horse?
Fast food.

Why did the colt gain weight?
He ate like a horse.

What's a horse's favorite state?
  Mare-land.

Why did the horse sleep all day?
  Because she was a nightmare.

Why did the horse turn in circles?
  He was just horsing around.

What's a motto for horses?
  If the horseshoe fits, wear it.

Why did the horse carry a big club?
  He was told to hit the hay.

Why are horses so negative?
  They say "neigh."

What do you call horses in adjoining stalls?
  Neigh-bors.

What do you call five giraffes?
  A high-five.

Who won the giraffes' race?
  It was neck and neck.

Where do giraffes get an education?
  In high schools.

What's a giraffe's favorite food?
  Neck-tarines.

What do you call a giraffe's relatives?
  Her necks of kin.

Where do giraffes live?
  In a high rise.

What do you call a thirsty giraffe?
  High and dry.

Which giraffes have the shortest necks?
The smallest giraffes.

Why aren't giraffes allowed to drive cars?
They create giraffic jams.

What's a giraffe's favorite movie?
Giraffic Park.

What do you call a giraffe's private country club?
High society.

How do camels hide in the desert?
They wear camel-flage.

What do you get if you cross a camel and
a dump truck?
Humpty Dumpty.

9
Critters with Wings

Why did the robin get a perm?
She thought the curly bird catches the worm.

Why was the bird arrested?
Because he was a robin.

What do you call a robin in an orange jumpsuit and handcuffs?
A jailbird.

Why did the jailbird want to catch the measles?
So he could break out.

What do you call a royal robin?
Lord of the Sings.

What do you get if you cross Little Red Riding Hood and a bird?
Robin Hood.

What shipwrecked bird was stranded on an island?
Robin Crusoe.

Why couldn't the bird chirp?
He had an untweetable illness.

Where do birds keep their money?
In the stork market.

How do birds dance?
They just wing it.

70

What do you call a parrot that likes to hike?
A walkie-talkie.

Why do parrots go to rock concerts?
Birds of a feather rock together.

Why did the baseball player wear a parrot on his head?
He wanted a feather in his cap.

What game do parrots play?
Hide and speak.

What do you call a missing parrot?
A polygon.

What do you get when a parrot swallows a clock?
  Polytics.

Where do young owls go for day care?
  To a hootenanny.

What did the mother owl say to her baby?
  "Owl always love you."

What do you call an elderly owl?
  An old coot hoot.

What's an owl's favorite subject?
  Owl-gebra.

Why was the owl different?
  He didn't give a hoot.

Why did the bird open a wig shop?
  Because he was a bald eagle.

What happens to a bee that lands
in a bowl of salad?
  Bee who hesitates is tossed.

Who is a bee's favorite singer?
  Sting.

Why didn't the bee commute to work on time?
His buzz was late.

What did the bee say in the sauna?
"Swarm in here."

What bee is very smart?
A spelling bee.

What does an annoyed bee say?
"Buzz off!"

What do you call an awkward bee?
A fumblebee.

What do you call a bee with a hard-to-hear buzz?
A mumblebee.

What did the bee tell her children?
"Bee-have yourselves!"

Who is a bee's favorite music composer?
Bee-thoven

How do bees stay warm?
They wear yellow jackets.

Where does a queen bee live?
In Bug-ingham Palace

What do you call a bee that cannot make
a decision?
   A may-bee.

What's yellow and black and goes in circles?
   A bee on a merry-go-round.

What happened to a bee on Halloween?
   He was bee-witched.

What's a bee's favorite flower?
A bee-gonia.

What does a bee say to a flower?
"Hello, honey."

Why do bees have sticky hair?
Because they use honeycombs.

What's a bee's favorite song?
Stinging in the Rain.

Where does the bee work?
He has his own buzzness.

Where do you find Asian bees?
In Stingapore.

What do you call a dance performed
by nervous insects?
The jitterybug.

What kind of hat does a bee wear?
A bee-nie.

Why can't bees win races?
They are always bee-hind.

What did a bee say to his girlfriend?
"You are bee-utiful."

What do bees chew?
Bumblegum.

10
Feathered Barnyard Critters

What happens when ducks tell jokes?
They quack up.

What game do ducklings play?
Quack the whip.

What do you get if you cross a duck
and a fireman?
  A firequacker.

What do you call two ducks named Jack?
  Quacker Jacks.

How does a duck read a secret message?
  He quacks the code.

What's a duck's favorite food?
  Cheese and quackers.

What do you get if you cross a duck
and a vampire?
  Count Quack-ula.

Why do ducks avoid doctor ducks?
  Because they are all quacks.

What kind of TV programs do ducks watch?
  Duckumentaries.

What grows down as they grow up?
  Ducks and geese.

What do you see when an overweight duck ice skates?

   A *quack in the ice.*

What do you get if you cross a flowerpot and a duck?

   A *quackpot.*

What do you call ducks in a cardboard carton?
A box of quackers.

What do you call a duck that makes funny remarks?
A wisequacker.

How do ducks make repairs?
They use duck tape.

What do you get if you cross a duck and a parrot?
An animal that says, "Polly wants a quacker!"

What do you get if you cross a chicken and a puppy?
The chick of the litter.

What happened when the chicken's fiancé called off their wedding?
She was madder than a wed hen.

What do you get if you cross a hen and a firecracker?
An eggsplosion.

What game do young chicks play?
Hide and peep.

Why are chickens smart?
They read hencyclopedias.

Why were the chickens arrested?
They were suspected of fowl play.

What do you get if you shake a chicken?
Scrambled eggs.

What do you get from evil chickens?
Deviled eggs.

What do you get if you cross a chicken and a dog?
Pooched eggs.

How do chickens dance?
Chick to chick.

Why did the chicken go to a psychologist?
She had a fear of frying.

What's a hen's favorite food?
Eggplant.

What do you call a nutty chicken?
  A cuckoo cluck.

Which hen is the first one awake each morning?
  The alarm cluck.

What do you get if you cross a chicken and a fish?
Cluckleberry Finn.

When do hens tiptoe?
When they are walking on eggshells.

How do chickens use math?
They count their chickens before they're hatched.

Why did the chicken cross the road twice?
She was a double-crosser.

Why is it easy for chickens to find jobs?
Because they work for chicken feed.

Why was the chick punished?
Because of his fowl language.

What's a chicken's favorite subject?
Eggonomics.

What do you serve chickens at a party?
Coopcakes.

On what day of the week do chickens hide?
Fry-day.

What did the hen tell her chick?
"You were a good egg."

Why did the hen go to the doctor?
For an eggsamination.

How do roosters greet each other?
"How do you doodle-do?"

How did the rooster escape from jail?
He flew the coop.

What do you get if you cross a rooster
and a crocodile?
A croc-a-doodle-do.

Why did the turkey cross the road?
To prove he wasn't a chicken.

Why do turkeys eat quickly?
Because they are gobblers.

What do turkeys have that other animals
do not have?
Baby turkeys.

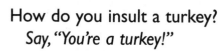

How do you insult a turkey?
Say, "You're a turkey!"

What holiday do turkeys celebrate?
  The Day After Thanksgiving.

How do turkeys break bad habits?
  They stop cold turkey.

What do you get if you cross a turkey
and an apple?
  An apple gobbler.

11
How Do Critters Say Good-bye?

Whale: "Sea you soon."

Snake: "Sssso long."

Bee: "I'm buzzing off."

Cat: "Have a mice day."

Big Cat: "I'll drop you a lion."

Bird: "Gotta fly."

12
Other Critter
Good-byes

"Ewe will be missed."

"I'll moose you, too."

"I'll miss each of you bear-y much."

"Howl soon will you be back?"

"Owl see you later."

"I'm otter here!"

Index